THE GREAT FAMILY

by Jerome W. Berryman

Illustrated by Lois Mitchell

Morehouse Education Resources,
a division of Church Publishing Incorporated
Editorial Offices: 600 Grant Street, Suite 630, Denver, CO 80203

For catalogs and orders call:
1-800-672-1789
www.Cokesbury.com

ISBN-13: 978-1-60674-196-2

Jerome W. Berryman:

To the Children of the world,

and for Thea, once again and always,
with gratitude...

Lois Mitchell

Dedicated to Katie B. and her family.

This is a story that takes place in the desert.
The trouble is that a real desert is too big to squeeze into a small book.
Sand would spill out everywhere,
so we will use only a little sand in a beautiful glass box to tell the story.
There are also too many people, so we will begin with just a few wooden figures.

In the desert the sand is always moving in the wind,
so it is hard to know where you are.
The blowing sand stings your face and hands.
There is almost no water in the desert,
so there is little to eat or drink.
In the daytime the sun scorches your skin and at night it is cold.
People do not go into the desert unless they have to.

The Great Family

After the great flood Noah led all the animals out of the ark.
They spread out in all directions to fill the earth with life again.
Some of the people gathered along the rivers.
They lived in small villages and then cities.
One of the greatest of these cities was Ur, a city near two rivers.

The people of Ur believed that there was a god in every tree,
rock or flower. The world was alive with gods!
This was a way to say the earth was holy,
but isn't God bigger than that?

There was a family in Ur that thought there was one God
who was everywhere!
This God created everything,
so *all of God* was in every place.
Abram and Sarai were part of this family.

One day the family of Abram and Sarai decided
they had to go to a new place.
They wondered what it would be like.
Would God really be there waiting for them?
The whole family set out across the desert,
even the animals.
They slept in tents at night, and
during the day the river showed
them the way and gave them
water to drink.
Finally, they met people coming out
from the new place, so they
knew their journey was
almost over.

The family settled in the small city of Haran.
They were happy, but sometimes in the evenings
Abram would go out into the desert.
He looked out across the sand and up into the sky.
One time God came so close to Abram,
and Abram came so close to God,
that he knew what God wanted him to do.
God wanted Abram and Sarai to go to *another* new place.
God blessed Abram to be a blessing.

The Great Family

Abram and Sarai went.
They said good-by to their family and set out, like God said.
This time there was no river to show them where to go
or give them water to drink,
but they found their way across the sand.

One day they came to a place called Shechem.
Would God be in this place, too?
Abram climbed a hill to pray.
God was there,
so they built an altar to mark the place
and moved on.

Next they came to Bethel.
Abram prayed again, and God was also there.
Now they *knew* that all of God was everywhere!
They built another altar and moved on once more.
When they came to Hebron,
they pitched their tent near the oaks of Mamre
and made their home there.

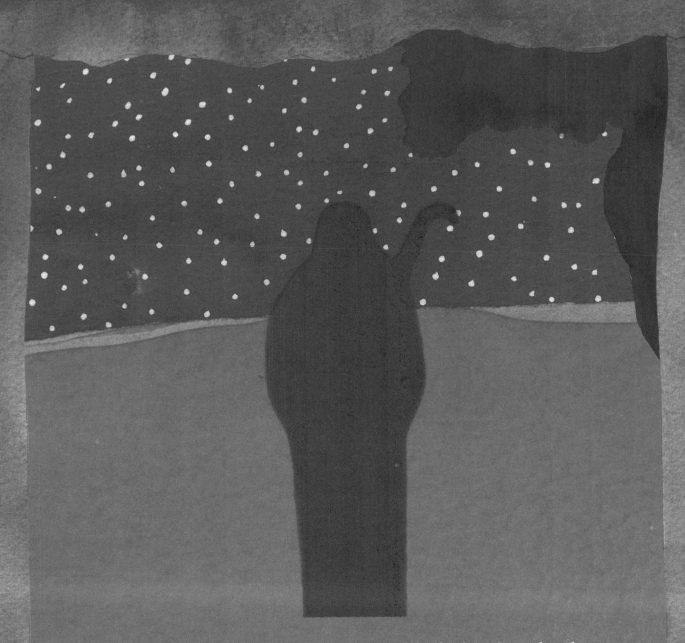

One night Abram went outside the tent and looked up into the sky.
God came so close to him, and Abram came so close to God,
that he knew what God was saying, even if no one else could hear.
"You will become the father of a great family
and Sarai will be the mother.
There will be as many in this family as there are stars in the sky.
This is why you will now be called Abraham and Sarah."

Abraham laughed so hard he fell down. Was God joking?
How could he and Sarah be the mother and father of a great family
when they had no children together of their own and were too old?

Sometime later three strangers
came out of the desert.
Abraham was sitting by his tent.
He invited them in and Sarah mixed
three measures of flour—which is a lot—
to make the bread to welcome them.
They said Abraham and Sarah would have a son!
Abraham laughed again, and this time Sarah,
who was standing nearby, laughed too.
The three strangers went on their way,
but do you know what happened?

The Great Family

Abraham and Sarah had a son.
They laughed a new laugh. It was the laughter of happiness.
Their laughing was not against God anymore.
It was with God, so they named their son "Laughter,"
which in their language was the name "Isaac."

The Great Family

Isaac grew and became strong,
but Sarah grew older and became weak.
One day she was too weak to go on and died.
One of the people who lived nearby
offered to give Abraham a place to bury Sarah,
but Abraham wanted to pay for the land anyway.
Sarah was buried in a warm cave near
the oaks of Mamre.

Abraham was very lonely.
He and Sarah had lived together for so many years.
It was hard to go on without her,
but he had one more thing he had to do.
He sent his most trusted helper back
to the land of his people
to find a wife for Isaac.

Abraham's helper crossed the desert and
one afternoon stopped by a well
at the end of his journey.
Rebekah was there and offered him some water to drink.
Then she helped him give water to his animals.
Rebekah was as full of courage as she was kind.
She invited him home, and he told her family
the story of The Great Family.

The Great Family

The Great Family

Rebekah listened carefully to the story
and decided she would like to be part of The Great Family.
She and Abraham's helper returned across the desert.
They walked past Shechem and Bethel
and finally came to Hebron.
Isaac saw them coming
and went out to meet them.
To everyone's delight,
Isaac and Rebekah were married.

The Great Family

The Great Family

Abraham was now *very* old
and so full of years that he too, died.
He was laid beside Sarah in the warm cave by the trees.

Isaac and Rebekah had twins.
And their children had children.
And those children had children.
This went on for thousands and thousands of years
until your grandmothers and grandfathers had children.
Then your mother and father had *you,*
so now you are part of The Great Family,
which has as many children as there are stars in the sky
and grains of sand in the desert.
And you? You are also blessed to be a blessing.

The Great Family

The Great Family

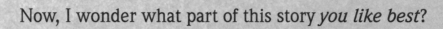

Now, I wonder what part of this story *you like best*?

34

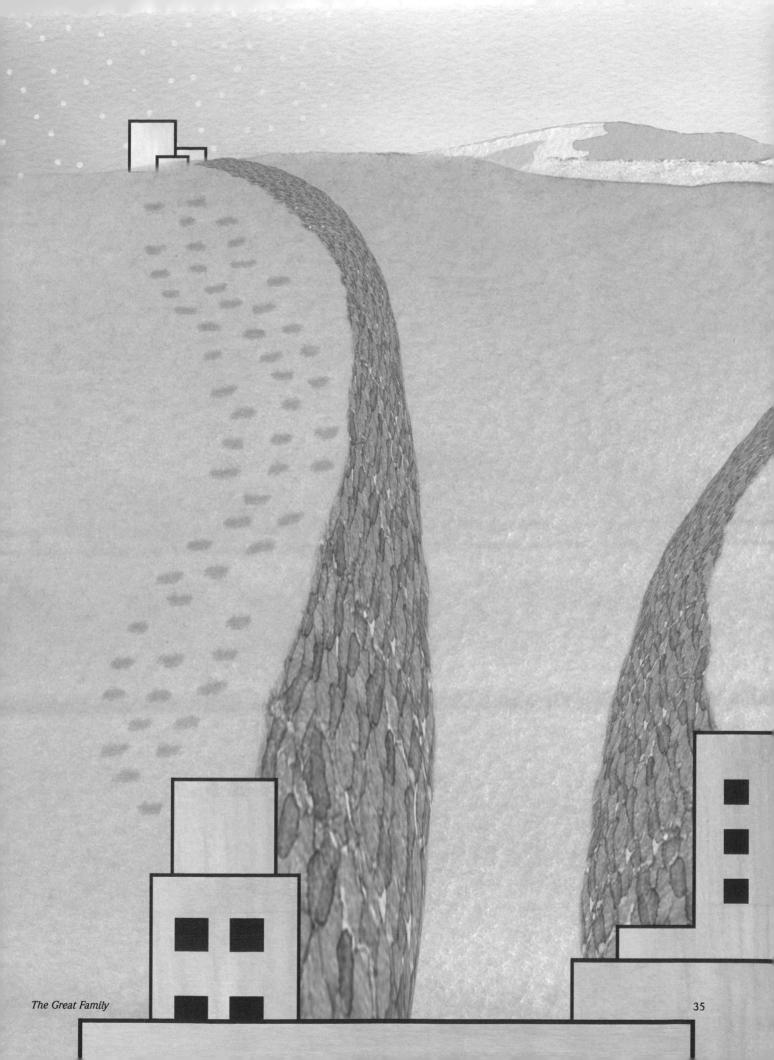

The Great Family

I wonder *what part* is the *most* important?

I wonder where *you* are in the story or what part of the story is about *you*?

I wonder if there is *any* part of the story we can *leave out* and still have all the story we need?

Printed in the USA
CPSIA information can be obtained
at www.ICGtesting.com
JSHW041935140824
68134JS00011B/123